First Facts™

Animal Behavior

Animals Raising Offspring

by Wendy Perkins

Capstone press

Mankato, Minnesota

First Facts is published by Capstone Press
151 Good Counsel Drive, P.O. Box 669, Mankato, Minnesota 56002
http://www.capstonepress.com

Library of Congress Cataloging-in-Publication Data
Perkins, Wendy.
    Animals raising offspring / by Wendy Perkins.
    p. cm.—(First facts. Animal behavior)
    Summary: Simple text explains the varied ways in which such animals as kangaroos,
gray whales, and woodpeckers take care of their young.
    Includes bibliographical references (p. 23) and index.
    ISBN 0-7368-2510-X (hardcover)
    1. Parental behavior in animals—Juvenile literature. [1. Parental behavior in animals.
2. Animals—Infancy.] I. Title. II. Series.
QL762.P47 2004
591.56'3—dc22   2003016182

Editorial Credits
Erika L. Shores, editor; Jennifer Bergstrom, series designer; Wanda Winch, photo researcher;
    Eric Kudalis, product planning editor

Photo Credits
Archbold Biological Station, Florida/Glen Woolfenden, 16–17
Bruce Coleman Inc./Clem Haagner, 5; Jen and Des Bartlett, 20; John Shaw, 12; Kenneth W. Fink,
    14; Kirk Schlea, 13; Larry Allan, 10–11; Michael Fogden, 15; Wayne Lankinen, 8
Corbis/Theo Allofs, 6–7
DigitalVision/Gerry Ellis and Karl Ammann, cover; NatPhotos, 9
Dwight R. Kuhn, 19

**First Facts thanks Bernd Heinrich, Ph.D., Department of Biology, University
of Vermont in Burlington, Vermont, for reviewing this book.**

1 2 3 4 5 6 09 08 07 06 05 04

Table of Contents

Raising Meerkat Pups

A mother meerkat's pups are hungry. The pups are too young to leave their **den**. While their mother hunts, another meerkat watches the pups. This meerkat stays with the pups all day. At night, the mother meerkat returns. She brings the pups insects or lizards to eat.

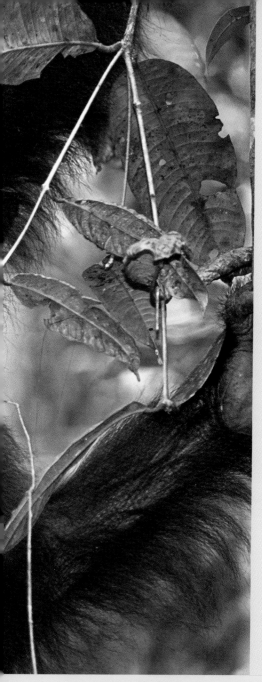

Growing Up

Animal **offspring** need time to grow into adults. Some animals care for themselves as soon as they are born. Other young animals need help from adults to **survive**. They need food and protection from **predators**. Animal offspring must learn how to get their own food.

 Fun Fact:
A young orangutan stays with its mother for seven to eight years.

Staying Safe

Predators often hunt young animals for food. Woodpeckers keep their chicks safe in a tree. Woodpeckers make a hole in a tree where their chicks stay.

A female kangaroo carries its
offspring in a pouch. The young
kangaroo is safe from predators there.

Feeding Offspring

Many animal offspring cannot find food on their own. Wolf pups eat food brought to them by other wolves in the pack. An adult wolf first chews the meat. It then spits out the small pieces of meat. The pups lick up the soft meat from the ground.

 Fun Fact:
All members of a wolf pack feed and play with the pups.

Learning to Live

Parents teach young animals how to find food. Young cheetahs stay with their mothers for about two years. The mother cheetah teaches them how to hunt.

A gray whale **calf** spends its first year
traveling with its mother. The mother
whale shows the calf where to find food.

 Fun Fact:
California gray whales travel about
10,000 miles (16,000 kilometers) each year.

Caring Fathers

Some male animals work hard to care for their offspring. A male emu sits on eggs laid by the female. The male emu also cares for the chicks after they **hatch**.

A male Darwin frog carries its young
in a mouth **sac**. The **tadpoles** leave their
father's mouth after they turn into frogs.

 **Fun Fact:**
A female Darwin frog lays about 30 eggs. After the eggs
hatch, the male Darwin frog puts the tadpoles in his mouth.

Helpful Families

Families help some animals raise their offspring. Scrub jays stay close to their parents. When new chicks hatch, young scrub jays help care for their brothers and sisters.

Raising Offspring

Many animals work hard to feed their offspring and keep them safe. Kangaroos carry their offspring in a pouch. Cheetahs teach their offspring how to hunt. Scrub jays work together to raise young. How do robins care for their offspring?

Amazing But True!

The male desert sand grouse flies many miles each day to find water. It soaks its body in water. The grouse then flies back to its nest. Young chicks drink the water from their father's feathers.

Hands On: Sniffing Scents

Some animals raise their offspring with the offspring of other animals. Parents can tell their offspring apart by the young animals' scents. Try this experiment to see if you can tell the difference between scents.

What You Need

two cotton balls

vanilla extract

eight paper cups

two cinnamon sticks

two whole cloves

two pieces of orange peel

wax paper or aluminum foil

eight rubber bands

pen or pencil

What You Do

1. Wet the cotton balls with some vanilla extract.
2. Drop a single cotton ball in two cups.
3. Place the cinnamon in two new cups. Place the clove in two new cups. Put the orange peel pieces in the remaining two cups.
4. Cover each cup with wax paper or aluminum foil. Use a rubber band to keep the cover on the cup.
5. Mark the bottom of each cup so you know what is inside.
6. Use the pen or pencil to poke five small holes in the cover.
7. Close your eyes and move all the cups around so they are mixed up.
8. Try to match the cups using only your sense of smell.

Glossary

calf (KAF)—a young whale

den (DEN)—the home where a wild animal lives

hatch (HACH)—to break out of an egg

offspring (OF-spring)—animals born to a set of parents

predator (PRED-uh-tur)—an animal that hunts other animals for food

sac (SAK)—a part of an animal that is shaped like a pocket or bag

survive (sur-VIVE)—to continue to live

tadpole (TAD-pohl)—the stage of a frog's growth between the egg and adult frog stages

Read More

Renne. *Young Animals and Their Parents.* Animals Up Close. Milwaukee: Gareth Stevens, 2000.

Stone, Tanya Lee. *Kangaroos.* Wild Wild World. San Diego: Blackbirch Press, 2003.

Internet Sites

FactHound offers a safe, fun way to find Internet sites related to this book. All of the sites on FactHound have been researched by our staff.

Here's how:
1. Visit *www.facthound.com*
2. Type in this special code **073682510X** for age-appropriate sites. Or enter a search word related to this book for a more general search.
3. Click on the Fetch It button.

FactHound will fetch the best sites for you!

Index